World Cultures: Ethiopia

By Jackie Chase

World Cultures: Ethiopia

Jackie Chase

WorldTravelDiva.com

CulturesOfTheWorld.com

World Cultures: Ethiopia
By Jackie Chase
AdventureTravelPress.com, Lady Lake, FL 32159
Copyright 2014 Jackie Chase
All rights reserved. Published 2014

Printed in the United States of America
Color Print: ISBN- 978-1-937630-78-2
E-book: ISBN- 978-1-937630-77-5

Library of Congress Cataloging
Travel

WorldTravelDiva.com
CulturesOfTheWorld.com

Other books by Jackie Chase

Winner of Royal Palm Literary Award, National Indie Excellence Awards, and Beverly Hills Book Awards

"100 People to Meet Before You Die" Travel to Exotic Cultures

"All Hands Working Together" Cruise for a Week: Meet 79 Cultures

"How To Become An Escape Artist" A Traveler's Handbook

"Giraffe-Neck Girl" Make Friends with a Different Culture

"Walking to Woot" Mom and Teen Bond in Primitive Culture (fall, 2014)

Prologue to Jackie's "singles" series

"Only those who risk going too far can possibly find out how far they can go."
T.S. Eliot.

Specially printed in color, and accessible with stunning back-lit color images as a bargain e-Book, this "single" recounts the adventures of Jackie Chase in Ethiopia. For her fans, the anthology of travels to 12 countries titled, "100 People to Meet Before You Die" Travel to Exotic Cultures contains many of the images from this "single" and eleven equally fascinating stories from cultures around the world.

Have you ever thought about becoming the hero of your own life story? On the horizon, there exists an invisible line between reality and our dreams. Have you had a yearning to ride by camel, experiencing saddle sores and searing heat, in order to know first-hand the life lived by nomadic desert tribes in Mali? Would you relish crawling through snakes disguised as vines in the steamy jungles of New Guinea to share huts with former headhunting warriors, while preparing your mind for sights that include dances you will never see on Broadway? Perhaps your love of water tempts you to consider the tranquility of remote rivers, accessible by a lone canoe, where tree sloths sleep for days. Or does your kind of adventure include visiting a regime where your attempted email gets intercepted by the government and never reaches home to say you survived OK, but you know you'll see village life that few foreigners can witness?

Does the China you crave require renting a bicycle because the transportation to remote villages by other means does not exist? Do you prefer to move from place to place by elephant, allowing for participation in the local scene? What if your fearless SUV driver maneuvered your vehicle into the virgin jungles of Ethiopia in order for you to stare down the AK-47s guarding the privacy of native tribes who seldom see a white-skinned woman, sacrificing the entire exterior of the vehicle to gunfire in the process?

Or do your milder moments cause you to dream of Bali, the perfect island, where the religion has evolved over many centuries, and the princedoms which exist today allow you to stay for less than $100 per night in the palace compound with the prince, a man descended from a continuous line of ancestors over 800 years?

If any of these experiences pique your adventurous spirit, then perhaps this "single" and the others in this series, or the anthology with its 321 photo stories of life in the world's villages could guide your planning for your next vacation.

On the other hand, you might like to experience the same thrills through the eye of the author's camera and her penciled journal notes while relaxing in your cozy home. You may wish to have a personal encounter with new friends that you never thought you could meet. These stories suggest both the primitive and the comfortable path to knowing and understanding cultures whose fascinating traditions may soon succumb to the tsunami of modern influences. Whether curled up in a hammock on an Amazon riverboat, or in the safety of your favorite armchair, accept the infection of the travel bug with enthusiasm and understanding. Reading this book can fill your opened mind with the enticing riches of our world and make the case for immersion in cultures that will do away with preconceptions and prejudice. Each of you, at little expense, can vicariously travel to exotic cultures as you live inside these pages. [Please remember, this is not an anthropology text or a complete guide to travel in each of these areas. It is the author's experience shared with you as a reporter of her journeys. These adventures are available on the web as singles, beginning with the words "World Cultures" and the name of the country, and this book is available in print with stunning color images In electronic download form, this, and other books by the author, can be ordered from all e-book sources. Images from this and other books are available for framing in many sizes upon request. Ask for the catalogue at Publisher@AdventureTravelPress.com]

World Cultures: A Series of Fascinating True Stories

List of "singles" by Jackie Chase

Blog: WorldTravelDiva.com (see updates/new books)

Website: CulturesOfTheWorld.com

[Available in color in print and eBook format]

World Cultures: Bali

World Cultures: Borneo

World Cultures: Burma

World Cultures: China

World Cultures: Ecuador

World Cultures: Ethiopia

World Cultures: India

World Cultures: Kenya

World Cultures: Morocco

World Cultures: Panama

World Cultures: Sulawesi

World Cultures: Vietnam

World Cultures: Ethiopia

"Not I nor anyone else can travel that road for you. You must travel it for yourself."   Walt Whitman.

Paint a picture of a dry desert with starving people, and Ethiopia comes to mind. Ethiopia, one of the most compelling countries in Africa, opens pathways that allow us to step back in time.

The word "history" found its initial breath millions of years ago with the first human remains unearthed near the capital, Addis Abba. Away from the scramble of city life, ripples of vivid lime to dark pine feed the eye.

Tourists interested in the Christian monuments and rock-hewn churches of the north wander the ancient alleyways lost in the fifteenth century. Halfway around the world, Ethiopia's geography and culture feel eons away from the wheat fields of Kansas.

Twice the size of Texas, Ethiopia offers geographical variety, with altitudes ranging from below sea level to heights of 4620m/15,000ft, creating one of the hottest places on earth, giving Ethiopia the nickname of "Roof of Africa."

Looking for an anthropological expedition? Make contact with primitive tribes in the southwest, the richest concentration of aboriginal tribes in the entirety of Africa.

These primitive tribes share ethics, values, and goals of non-materialistic traditions.

Compensated with the symbolic and ornamental wealth on their embellished bodies, people live satisfied and balanced lives.

1. Hammer tribal planting corn

Variations of traditions range from the practical to the exotic in the population of rural villages. The environment dictates simplicity and practicality in living quarters, like small mud huts with grass tops for the nomadic or semi-nomadic tribes. Animal skins embellished with shells and bottle caps cover bodies coated in red paint for decoration, with hairstyles I'll leave to the imagination. A natural affinity for beauty gives the Ethiopians a reason for breathtaking clothing, hairstyles, and, most of all, jewelry. The Ethiopians pursue a heritage that remains vital to their cultural ethics and religious rituals, often reflected in their garments and style.

2. Tsamy walking from Konso wearing animal skins

The Mursi, Hammer, Karo, Konso, Galeb, and Borana tribes all co-exist in a cracked and craggy environment, forgotten by the rest of the world.

Here, the visitor can see the Africa of yesterday. In their hidden cloisters, these tribesmen's symbolic customs flourish through body adornment. The power of nature dominates while strong ties link them to the Omo River as their main life source.

******

Green patches of maize, cotton, and sorghum, and villages, like little brown buttons separated by the stitching of fence borders, completed the seen-from-the-sky quilt.

In the center of each village, a yellow circle contained the second-hand of a clock ticking. While the plane sank from the sky, I could see cattle tied side-by-side, their bellies rubbing and their heads down, walking in a circle, grinding maze.

Baboon families scattered around the grass runway, a welcome end to the ten-passenger flight from Addis to Arba Minch, the beginning of my sojourn to villages not found on common maps.

Girma, my guide, driver, cook, friend, and interpreter, greeted me with a smiled sigh of relief after waiting two days for my flight, delayed for reasons that changed faster than the ripples on water.

My bag of tricks included the following: water purifier, enough cans of tuna to cause an overweight charge, a new tent tricking me into believing the waterproof tag, enough batteries to open a store, (though this did not help the new flashlight with the broken bulb), and lots of hope.

I arrived, ready to camp in the raw Africa that greeted me.

Girma promised a hotel of some sort if possible. For eight birr ($1), the first night's hotel consisted of an empty room with no screens. Malarial mosquitoes buzzed my neck, which meant setting up the tent inside the room.

Shutters and doors had broken locks or none at all. How could I squeeze all my gear, boots, and body into a one-man tent?

For further protection from the gang of mosquitoes waiting for a bare-skin feast, I left my long sleeves, pants, and socks on, and woke up drenched in sticky, wet perspiration from the intense heat of the closed-in space.

A bush in the jungle offered more privacy than the wood platform with a hole in the middle for a toilet.

3. Mursi without her lip disc.

The Mursi, one of the most peculiar native peoples of Ethiopia, live as herdsmen and warriors. Myths, symbols, and superstitions influence the Mursi's way of conveying their significance. Girls start their ritual mutilations around age ten to begin the process to achieve womanhood. Without drugs or modern tools, the Mursi extract the two, lower-incisor teeth to make room for the lip plates, a common tradition for the Mursi women.

Skilled women pierce the ears of teenagers for insertion of clay and wood disks. After the teen becomes fifteen, one of the women of her family makes an incision in her lower lip to allow for stretching of the opening until it is large enough for insertion of a small lip plate.

About six months before marriage, stretching continues with larger plates inserted into the pierced lip. The elasticity of the lip increases in time, allowing easy removal of the plates. Women must wear discs when men are present, but take them out when sleeping or eating alone.

The Mursi suggest three reasons for the adoption of the unnatural custom. Men believed the strange behavior would discourage slave traders from taking their women, the same reason the Palaung women wear brass rings around their necks in Thailand.

The superstitious believed the ugly discs kept evil spirits from entering the body. The size of the disc designates the bride price or number of cattle acceptable for the future wife's hand in marriage.

The woman, wearing many arm bracelets and large lip discs, demands maybe fifty cattle for her parents. Other traditions include scarification of the body and face along with wild-as-one's-imagination body paintings. These acts may attract the opposite sex.

Men compete for recognition of masculinity and strength. The young men love a sport called *donga,* or stick fighting. Winners earn status among their peers.

Some have the opportunity to win a girl's hand in marriage. Villages come together, and winning fighters challenge each other.

The aggressive reputation of the Mursi plagues outsiders, most often the Bana tribes, over disputes of trespassing, stolen cattle, or revenge for evil spells supposedly cast over their herds.

4. Carrying market purchase

5. Tribal man carrying his rifle

    South of the Mursi village, on the edge of the Mago National Park, lies the Village of Duss, home of the Karo people. An endangered people with less than a thousand surviving, the Karo do creative body paintings using available white chalk, pulverized iron ore, black charcoal, and yellow mineral rock. Women scarify their chests, as they believe the skin holds sensual appeal for men. They decorate animal skin coverings with cowrie shells, beads, soda bottle lids, and even the metal pop-top lids from soda cans. Villagers cut hair in a bowl shape and cover it in red clay. Both men and women pierce the lower lip to insert objects like small sticks or nails.

6. *Children playing in the market area*

Men spend much more time on their hairstyles. After a part to divide the hair in half, a man weaves the front section into braids to hang down over the forehead. He gathers the back section into a ball and covers it with a cap of mud. Holes punched in softened bark make spaces for ostrich feathers.

Men wash their bodies in ashes mixed with fat, which helps fight mosquitoes and the tsetse fly, and the ashes demonstrate virility in festivals and combats with neighboring clans. Scarification on a man's chest shows he has killed a dangerous animal or enemy. Using knives, razors, or sharp branches, they cut the flesh and later rub ash into the wounds to cause the scars to swell. Former nomads, the Karo, differ from all other groups around the Omo River as they have settled in one village. A Karo man may take as many wives as he can afford, but often settles for two or three.

******

Mangled pieces of the bridge lie visible on the river bottom. A construction worker yelled something in foreign words, which my driver translated, "You can cross the River Omo in your four-wheel to reach the Mursi Village."

Halfway across the swift current the Amharic word for "help" echoed through the jungle. I wondered if I should have believed the email from the agency hiring my driver, telling me to abort the Mursi trip. Due to El Nino's harsh side effects, previous clients had to leave the area by helicopter, and I feared now that I might follow them out of this country in the same way.

The worker transferred the chain from a metal bridge railing to our Land Cruiser and hopped into a nearby tractor, shouting at it as he coaxed it forward, pulling our vehicle behind it. My driver, Girma, explained, "We will try an opening in the jungle down the road leading to the village where the Mursi women with their five-inch clay-lip-disks live."

7. Lip disc on Mursi woman

   Within minutes, the jungle branches, vines, and insects stuck to the car like honey. I had to give up trying to wipe away the constant salty trickles of sweat, blurring my vision. I was using up my toilet paper for the job, and toilet paper is a much-needed necessity for other purposes.

Intense humidity and high temperatures shut down both the air conditioner and our hopes of reaching the mysterious Mursi people. With the windows closed for protection from the clawing vines and hordes of black biting flies, we gave our attention to the dry, riverbed crevices we had to maneuver.

A familiar smell distracted me from my watch for problems ahead. My concerns changed course after seeing the back and side windows covered in something oily and wet. Girma ignored my questions about the smell while slowing for two men wearing skimpy loincloths and shouldering AK47s. Girma tried to rationalize his reason for allowing the men to ride with us by saying, "The men will help build temporary, tree-branch bridges for the tires where the jungle has given way to the flooding waters."

The doors held tight by the wild and free jungle meant the men had to climb in through the driver's-side window. Both men climbed over the front seat awkwardly, with private parts flopping about. Their hands clenched the headrests so hard their skin turned white, and I could almost hear one man's jaw drop down to his belly with anxiety at seeing his surroundings. In and out of the window, the two men and Girma climbed in order to cut tree branches to connect the wide openings.

Minutes later, three naked men with Kalashnikovs, also called Russian AK-47 semi-automatic rifles, stood with perfect posture behind a fallen tree, stationed there to protest our passing. Adventure travel put to the test! Spirited, naked men waving rifles? Girma wrinkled his eyebrows as if to question my concern. Truckloads of these rifles cross the border from Sudan and Somalia. Locals increase their status when they carry a gun rather than a spear. My driver offered them a few coins, and they disappeared before a river stopped the vehicle once again. The Mursi people have a reputation for demanding money and food.

"When we reach the river close to their village," Girma said, "we will wait for them to visit us. Their curiosity levels match ours; plus they hope to receive some money for showing off their lip plates and painted naked bodies." Girma spoke as if he had memorized the words before the trip.

Most of the villagers materialized like whispering aliens, and the women pulled their loose lip-skin out and around clay disks. Shiny ebony bodies appeared from behind trees, crossing the shallow river toward us. I knew they could hear my heart beating fast and could sense my fear. My dream of crossing the boundaries of the civilized stood before me, embodied in these people, tugging at my hair, shirt pockets, and camera strap. Rough pieces of tree bark had rubbed their bodies clean of hair. Intricate white designs hid the nakedness of those bodies. The sun played with the metal decorating the animal-skin loincloths on the women.

A woman came close and stood still as if to offer herself for a photo. I snapped a few pictures. She took the lip plate out of her lip, offered it to me and held up her fingers. Girma said she wanted a ten-birr note ($.80). I knew I had to pay for every photograph when they increased the number of fingers held up with each click. The tribes understood the reason for my presence. If I could reward these people for giving me their time while continuing their traditional ways, perhaps in some small way I could contribute to the preservation of their culture. But sometimes the tribes took advantage of strangers due to some tourists tossing hundred-birr notes ($8) at them for a couple of photos.

Tribals soon learn the value of money and expect the next visitor to pay the same. When the tourists say no, dangerous situations occur. And that's what happened to me and Girma that day. An argument started between two women and a man. Apparently, the man thought he might miss some payment since I took a photo of the woman who was not his wife. After a half hour of trying to communicate with my driver and watching my photography antics, the Mursi chief asked Girma for the equivalent of twenty dollars.

A group of men circled the car waving spears and rifles. Girma reached for two boxes of crackers to pass out and, with caution, opened the car door. I followed his actions. A live encounter with the Mursi tribe could provide a frightening experience not worth the effort of getting there. Leaving under this kind of stress caused a sensation of needles pricking my arms and face. Burning, salty sweat kept me from seeing the real aggression in the Mursis' eyes.

The driver ignored the crowd around the vehicle while creeping forward. Dead ahead, the three naked men, now wearing loincloths, pointed the guns in our direction while standing again behind another dead tree. They caught the *birr,* or Ethiopian currency, in midair as Girma tossed it toward them and proceeded around the dead tree. The driver explained that last week they had killed a park scout! We searched for the dip in the tree canopy, evidence of the previous tree felling.

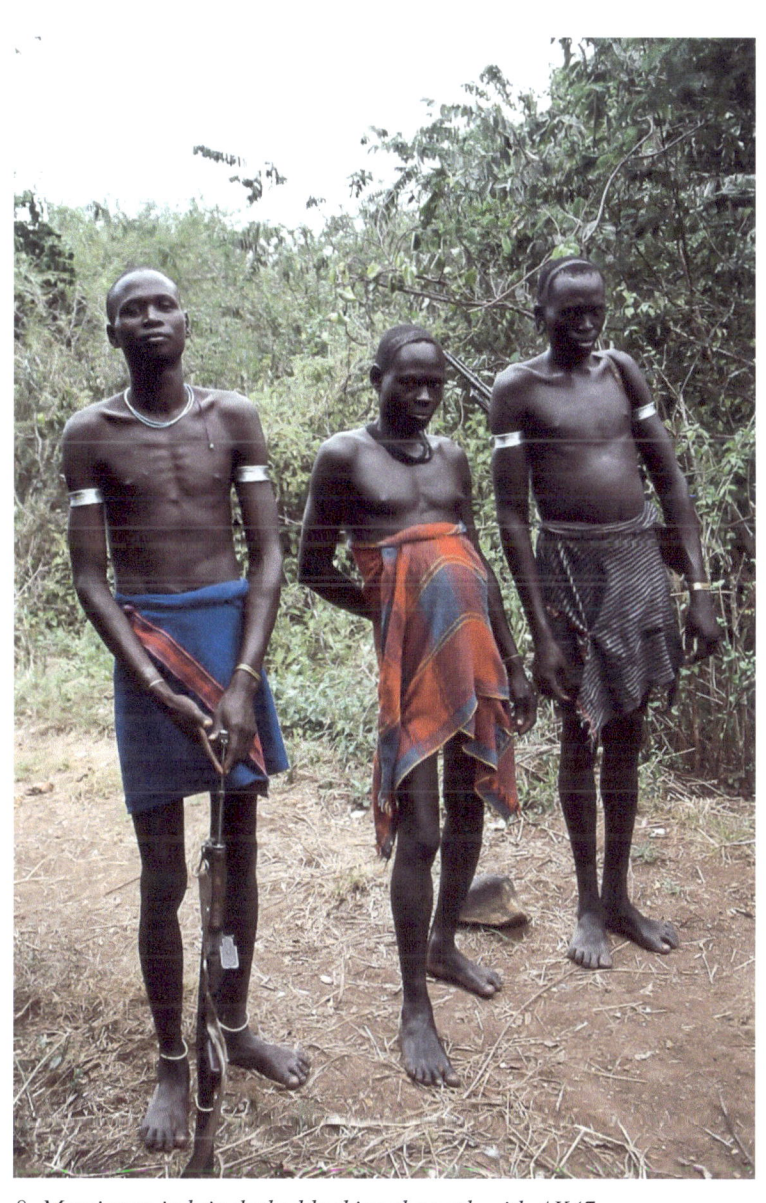
8. Mursi men in loincloths blocking the path with AK47s

9. *Mursi playing handmade musical instrument*

10. Young girls selling gourds

    A rough, dirt road never looked so good until we left the car for some fresh air. With tears in his eyes, my young driver circled the clawed, dented, and diesel-fuel-covered car. The jungle growth had worked hard to try to keep the vehicle from entering its playground. Headlights, taillights, bumpers, and trim pieces looked like an angry weightlifter had slammed his heaviest weights at the vehicle. Thorn bushes fought with broken branches, competing for the challenge of leaving their imprint of black, horizontal stripes across every door. All of the five-gallon, diesel-fuel containers remained tied to the misshapen luggage rack, crushed to a fourth of their original size. Three weeks of fuel washed the car while we dealt with men with guns.

11. Galeb tribal dressed in animal skins

12. Digging for water in a dry riverbed

I never thought much about what might have happened to us, nor at the time did I worry when I saw the almost ferocious look on the men's faces, as they gathered around the 4X4, chanting for money. Traveling to meet indigenous societies requires a vast amount of trust and patience for one's driver and all of humankind. If some gypsy could have predicted that situation beforehand, perhaps I would have thought twice about trying to find the Mursi.

******

Drinking very hot bottled water while eating peanut butter on rolls, both Girma and I reflected on the events with the Mursi, the battered vehicle, and our own exhaustion. Girma laughed, saying the small river had dried up, and his earlier promises to me of a cool river to dip in would have to wait. Covered in sweat, leaves, dead bugs and dust, I pinched him as we stopped on the banks of a muddy stream. Cooling off, although not cleaning off, triggered my joyful splash into the water, heard for miles around.

Not an hour into the flat scrub bush jungle, I saw smoke. Girma called it the "Devils Wind" and kept driving toward it. If it's like a tornado, why drive into it? Topping a hill, our vehicle faced hordes of animals racing fast enough to beat the red-hot flames, grumbling and hissing. Dead savannah grass, the underbrush of the thickets, and thorny Acacia trees, fed the fire as fast as it could consume them. The sandy clearing offered little help for turning around until Girma shifted into four-wheel drive. Their "interstate system" consists of dry riverbeds and sometimes a cattle trail.

13. Cooking inside hut

Girma said, "No need to warn the park rangers. They can do nothing to stop the fire, so we will turn around and go back to Jinka for more fuel and then travel down to the villages of Demeka and Turmi to meet the Bana and Hammar peoples."

Looking back, I noticed the two red spots of flames blended into one long line of red. Fifteen minutes later sprinkles cleared our car of the dusty day, while giving the fire what it deserved!

14. Cooking oxen dung for food

15. Boy carving neck stools

Descending into the Great Rift Valley toward Kenya and Sudan meant leaving the shadowy treescapes and fertile cotton fields to head into the classical sandy earth and mud-colored brush. The remote location of Southern Ethiopia creates difficulties when the traveler attempts to find villages, as roads turn into dry, rocky riverbeds with no village in sight.

Ethiopians use the flour from *teff,* or staple grain, to bake *injera,* or large pancake-like breads, served on the table. Meats consist of muscle and gristle. The injera holds the food, and, using his or her fingers, diners tear off portions of *injera* and roll up food pieces. Did Girma miss eating his customary staple of *injera*?

16. Grinding maze on a stone

Camping in Ethiopia requires skills beyond those of the standard canoe trips of my college days in the Midwest. Thieves and baboons rank highest of the camper's concerns. Girma traced the edge of the windshield while explaining the best way for thieves to get into the vehicle without leaving notice. Later, when you miss your camera, documents, and hiking boots, you see evidence of the careful removal of the windshield glass. So even inside the car, you tie the equipment together with extra caution for hiding valuables.

Baboons look cute when six weeks old. I know. I babysat one owned by a pet shop owner. They live in large families and love to carry loose items away in the middle of their day (your night.) Nighttime trips to the jungle toilet will challenge your confidence even when attempted with an armed guard.

17. The leaky purple tent

A group of trees and bushes almost in a circle caught our attention as we searched for a suitable campsite. The oncoming dusk urged us to set up camp quickly, and I liked the enclosure, surrounded by this tree fence, and a football field's distance to the local government-placed well for bathing and cooking water. Tents in place, gear stored and locked tight, we took a quick walk through the nearby village before another boring spaghetti dinner. I introduced myself to the chief as he casually emptied his honey trap. Smoke, along with a smell so intrusive I had to pinch my nose, came from a black gourd balanced on a bed of black and red embers. The chief's son boiled oxen dung in a calabash, or oversized gourd, and added honey as the final ingredient before this spiritual liquid could bring good luck at dinner! In his hands, the young boy held a black ball. I never did ask or figure out its use or composition.

18. Wrapping bundles of firewood

When it comes to protecting my health on a fourth-world trip like this, my paranoia develops. Extensive research provided me with tips on boiling water for at least thirty minutes before use for cooking or drinking. The previous year my teenage daughter, Katherine, and I spent a month living with the Stone Age peoples of New Guinea and used this method of purifying water for all our tea made from muddy, brown, river water. We avoided any problems with sickness. I taught Girma that the thirty minutes starts after the bubbles appear. We played a timing game each day. After boiling the spaghetti and sprinkling it with instant tomatoes, he poured water direct from the well over the pasta! So much for a spaghetti dinner for me! Another empty can of tuna to bury with the rest of the garbage in the morning.

19. Tribal boys tasting author's leftover spaghetti for the first time

Girma insisted that tribal onlookers keep their distance and use the small opening into our camping circle as the stay-back line. To avoid wasting our excess spaghetti (the dry pasta expands with the moisture in the air), Girma invited some children who were peering into our camp to join him for dinner. Villagers, hoping for a glimpse into another world, hid behind bushes or gathered in groups to point at my weird clothing, boots, or wild, purple-and-pink tent. Girma showed the boys how to take a stick and wind the pasta around it, but they found it easier to shove it into their mouths with their fingers.

What fun watching pasta hanging from their mouths. Sharing western foods, I experience guilt, as I would prefer not to tempt these young minds with new ideas in the ways of living. This comedy caused us all to laugh with each bite taken!

Do not believe those ads that guarantee a sound and restful night sleeping on self-inflating, half-inch-thick, sleeping pads. Sticks and stones reminded me all night of my age and my growing dislike of camping while I lay on my too-thin pad.

Memories still return, as I recall the hours spent listening to those lions and colabus monkeys, who jumped trees faster than you could blink your eye.

The first time I tried to bathe created a scene, as I did not understand the traditions for using the well. This cement well, government-placed, had an open-ended trough so water rolled off the end.

With my shirt stretched out on the ground, I thought a sponge- bath sounded appealing, a chance to cool my body. Off came my shirt while I fidgeted with the pump.

Two young men appeared like ghosts and tried to take my place pumping the handle.

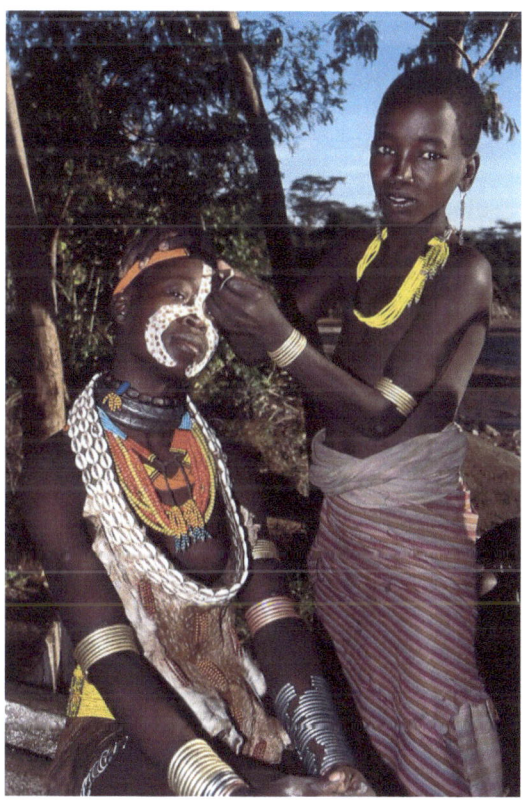

20. Painting faces at the well

"Go away, go away," I demanded, but their looks of bewilderment gave me reason to grab my shirt and run back to camp.

"Their custom becomes their duty. Men have the responsibility of pumping the handle and women gather the water. Those boys tried to help you," my guide told me.

I walked back to the well and found about eight kids chatting and giggling. My appearance changed the noise level to zero as they stared at this white-skinned woman in long pants and strange-looking boots. Besides, I was carrying a polyester camping towel and odd containers filled with white liquid.

My smiles gave them permission to get back to their face and body painting, using small twigs as brushes dipped in white chalk and red ochre powder. I soon faded to invisible, sitting on a clump of dead vines as I caught their fun on film.

Coffee plantations in the remote, high plateaus and my location, recorded by tiny landmarks on the GPS, turned into memories as the 4X4 sank its tires into knee-deep ruts. The last of the river water, abandoned by the crocodiles, made many canoes homeless. Nevertheless, the landscape grew thick with people, somehow surviving.

Termite nests, towering thirty feet above, provided shade for the Hamar people and offered a way to escape the sizzle of the desert heat. The unrelenting surroundings contribute to maintaining the ancient customs of exotic people like the Hamar in the area of Turmi.

Broad savannahs spotted with thorn bushes and cacti provide a harsh environment for the support of the Hamar's cattle.

Beekeeping and pottery keep hands busy, singing to soothe their cattle and. building fires at night to warm them. The Hamar live for their cattle. Young men move their cattle to grazing areas around the crocodile-infested waters of the Omo River.

When their roots and grains run out, they depend on cattle's milk and blood from the neck for survival. Packs of wild jackals or hyena, and cattle raiding threaten the lives of both the cattle and their young guardians.

Villagers measure a family's wealth by the number of cattle owned. Famine, drought, needing a few more cattle for a wedding dowry, or taking weapons of the men killed calls for cattle raiding.

Cattle serve as the Hamar's living bank account, and without cattle, a young man cannot get married, as a bride price can cost as much as fifty cattle.

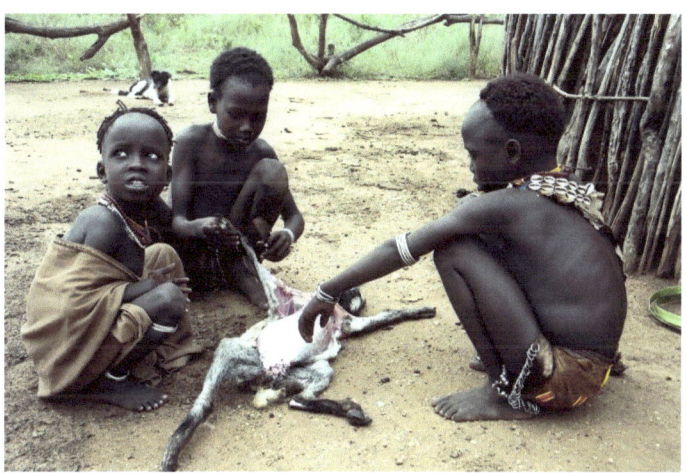

21. Turmi children skinning a goat for food

Part of the culture for these people includes raids to kill a man from another tribe. Killing, for ownership of water rights, for access to a prized lion, or to avenge the theft of cattle would cause the Mursi/Bana, the Karo/Bume or the Hammer/Galeb tribes to fight back and forth.

Men gain high status within communities for killing a man or large animal such as a buffalo, elephant, or lion. To kill a man takes less effort. Many warriors turn their backs on the traditional weapon, the spear.

The celebration for killing an enemy starts with the sacrifice of a goat for blood to wash away the man's guilt for having killed another man. A man cannot marry until he has killed an enemy or large game animal.

A significant part of the killing ritual involves scarification. The elders hire a scarrist when they can afford to hire one, and she cuts crude designs on the killer's upper body and uses the *garanti* plant, or dead spirits food, to heal the wound.

To reach manhood, the young boy has to pass the *bullah,* or bull-jumping ceremony. A dozen or more cattle are lined up, side by side, and covered in dung. Success in jumping up and running across all the cattle backs ensures the boy a new wife and tribal acceptance.

22. Hammar woman carrying a heavy load

Both male and female tribe members show their love for physical beauty through hair grooming.

Women rub fat and red ochre paint into their hair and wear it in *goscha,* or short ringlets.

Men who have killed a dangerous animal or enemy wear a cap made of mud. Softened bark with holes or tiny goat bones holds ostrich feathers.

Most men carry a *borkoto,* or carved stool, to protect their hairstyles. Carving their own borkotos, boys as young as eight sit in the markets.

Engaged or married women wear *essente,* or iron necklaces, which stay on their necks for a lifetime. A first wife carries a *binyere,* or phallic protrusion attached to the front of the necklace.

The village *garsho,* or blacksmith, closes the neck circles with a hammer and closes the arm and leg rings on the women. Years ago, twenty-five rings cost one cow.

If a woman dies before her husband, he removes the rings from her severed body parts so he can give them to his new wife.

23. Proud and beautiful tribal woman

A group of villagers hung around our campsite day and night, trying to sell me ancient artifacts belonging to deceased tribal members, or maybe hoping for a few birr notes for a photograph. A woman, bent in half from the heavy load on her back, stood watching, while Girma packed the 4X4, and I collapsed the tents. Two young boys, with smiles, inviting me to join them, helped the heavy-laden woman move her burdensome bags to the ground, ,. One pointed to her heavy brass bracelets that circled from her wrists to her elbows and pointed to my arm with questioning looks. Although I didn't say yes, he proceeded to pry open her bracelets one by one with a rock as each had a quarter-inch opening. After pounding and prying with the rock, he took his shoe made from a rubber tire and shoved it into the opening. He tugged so hard trying to separate the brass opening enough for her wrist to slip out that he broke his shoe in half. He squeezed her wrist out and mine in. The bracelets cling tight on the skin and don't move around, so he pushed them to my elbow and pounded them closed. By the time the opening for the ninth bracelet closed, the inside of my wrist had bled and some of the skin on my arm hung in bloody ribbons.

24. Oxen plowing

People die from infections in a tropical environment. I do not get paranoid with worry; otherwise,

I guess I would not have traveled to this wild, remote place, but the extra care these boys had taken with me caused me concern. The jewelry exhibits status and wealth. Rings worn from the wrist to the shoulders and on the legs could mean a high status in a village. The group exhibited pride as they stepped back to see my reaction. I did not understand why they shared this tradition with me, an outsider. I offered the woman some birr, and she shook her head. In a country of beggars, drought, and severe hardship, I wanted her somehow to know my appreciation for her friendship.

"Girma, do we have food we won't eat on this trip?" Two boxes of cornflakes took up space in the food box along with a large box of powdered milk. Hot milk with cornflakes sounded disgusting, so I asked him if I could give that to the woman in trade for the lifetime memories she gave me.

25. Selling gourds in tribal market

The Ethiopian government attempts to control tribal life. Federal officials work their influence to win the support of village chiefs in the hopes of abolishing all harmful traditional practices.

Government organizations prohibit certain practices like *Minga,* a belief that certain things bring bad luck. A child, born out of wedlock, deformed, or who had its front teeth grow in before its bottom teeth, will die of exposure after his mother abandons him in the forest, desert, or river.

Other regulations outlaw female circumcision, scarifications, piercings for lip plates, stick fighting, cattle jumping, and the whipping of women in ceremonies.

To witness these traditions, tourists spend their money to cross vast and uncomfortable distances.

26. Tribal friends gathered in market

27. Berber women bringing salt to market from Somalia

A few times on this trip, I have seen 4X4s with white-skinned people inside. Initially, I wondered where they camped, for some kind of reality check or means of pinching me to prove that I lived this dream.

Pausing, I asked myself if I felt lonesome or needed their company. Did I want to hear about events in the world spoken in English? I live on my computer back home like young people today live on their phones but the thought of checking email or wondering about world events didn't enter my mind here in this primitive place.

Meeting with unusual challenges, setting up campsites, visiting with the locals, and finding places to wash my clothing and body consumed my time and energy. Whether curious or begging, the tribal people and their constant attention drained me. Solo travel demands a great deal of patience.

Girma never seemed to leave me alone unless I made a point to tell him that I needed privacy in the bush. I don't think I ever felt loneliness in spite of this trip's exhausting physical and emotional demands.

28. Scraps patch worked into a hut

A timeless culture, colliding with modern day sensibilities, offered me a glimpse back in time through the living tribes I met in village after village.

29. Author talking with Galeb children

30. Karo sisters pumping water from a local Konso well

31. Karo girls shave their heads until they pass through puberty

32. Hammar teenager, with shaved head, resting in Demeka market

33. Painted faces

WHY TRAVEL?

"It is not necessarily at home that we best encounter our true selves." Alain de Botton

Is it the lure of an escape that makes one want to travel? Or does adventure lurk in the sounds of places like Kathmandu? Islands like Bora Bora and Bali conjure images of palm trees on deserted beaches and romance. An impulse of spontaneity in your life may cause you to make travel plans and the anticipation compares to getting ready for Christmas. Preparations, or the process of getting there, have rewards as enjoyable as reaching the destination. Have you made a promise to yourself that the mystery around the bend in the road ahead will merit your aspirations for getting there?

Travel offers challenges that increase with time.

"A journey of a thousand miles begins with a single step," according to a Chinese proverb.

The rewards of travel come from the journey of self-discovery. As you begin to make your own rules and learn to trust yourself, you begin to redefine your individualism.

"I had hoped that the trip would be the best of all journeys: a journey into ourselves." Shirley MacLaine

While traveling you will begin to experience the unexplainable change that will take place inside. Removing the masks of everyday life, you participate in someone else's journey by getting involved with their lives and looking at things in a different way. Ask about their customs, religion, food products, how they make a living, their pastimes for relaxing, what they view as important to them, and what they consider as their goals.

That exposure to more traditional customs causes you to change your own lifestyle. By taking these baby steps toward understanding, we remove the barriers we construct in our everyday life. We all wear masks, sometimes many at one time. Do we speak up to an employer when he's wrong, or do we hide behind our job security safety net and keep our feelings private? Do we dress differently when with a different set of friends? What do we say to a group of girlfriends at lunch when they talk about buying red cowboy boots, but you are thinking how odd they will look in them?

While traveling, nobody will judge you, and your body language will not identify you as mother, lawyer, best friend, Little League coach, boss, neighbor, or any other title.

"Are we the same people, I wonder, when all our surroundings, associations, acquaintances are changed?" Gertrude Bell, a Victorian explorer, once pondered.

Live the definition of serendipity! We often believe that our outer landscape serves as our strongest attribute, and we depend on our dress, manicures, and Botox; by feeding your soul, you realize that the inner landscape has great importance. By expanding your outer world, you'll make invisible inner changes that will last a lifetime.

The value of Tolkien's words, *"Not all those who wander are lost,"* begins to make sense. For a travel virgin, the highs and lows you encounter will complete your experience.

You will find your senses, personal habits, patience, attitude and capabilities tested to your limit. You will learn to respect the beauty of a people and their traditions from ancestors past, no matter how difficult it seems. The simplicity of a place may overwhelm you. No running water or electricity? The lack of motivation that concept creates will disappear when you are actually walking into a small Third-World village and witnessing the men sitting around singing while carving wooden musical instruments. By questioning these realities, you better understand your world. As you walk around with your iPod hanging out of your pocket, don't protest the authenticity of indigenous peoples living centuries-old customs. First, seek to understand before becoming judgmental.

Begin to challenge your abilities. Accomplishments you never dreamed possible will become second nature to you. Greet the unexpected with smiles and patience. All of your senses will ignite as you face decisions without computers, newspapers, and televisions with answers for the questions of How? What? Where? Your travels will act like a magnet, gathering experiences that will challenge your curiosity and provoke your questions. When you need to trust yourself for your answers, your fears and insecurities vanish, and the excitement comes as you witness a new you emerging.

We all have the traditional boundaries we make for ourselves as well as the ones others chart on maps and in guidebooks for us. By stepping over those roadblocks, we find we can do things we never dreamed possible. Maybe those rituals serve as a signpost along the road of a much bigger journey.

Riding on the roof of a train from Guayaquil, Ecuador with my fourteen-year-old daughter, I felt helpless when the train stopped without explanation in a town whose name we never knew. The village, off the tourist track, offered no hotels or food or even help to find our way onward. Half a mile up on the main road, I could see what I hoped were bus passengers gathered. Each passing bus held demanding mothers late in preparing dinner or fathers tired from a long day of fieldwork.

After I had shouted "Riobamba" over and again, the group realized my wishes to go north. A few hours passed, and the sun disappeared. A truck filled with green hard-as-rock bananas pulled up, and many from the group yelled to me, "Riobamba, Riobamba." Along with about ten other needy souls, my daughter and I climbed into the back of that truck, and within half an hour, we had taught songs to others journeying with us, shared our nuts and raisins, and wondered where we might land. I could sit on that dirt road all night with a young daughter or take my chances in a truck going somewhere. In my lifetime, I have never hitchhiked and never conceived of getting into a truck filled with strangers who spoke no English. When it started to rain, we pulled a huge tarp over the group and continued our songs and laughter. Within four hours, someone yelled "Riobamba!" We peeked out from under the tarp to see a washed-out sign that we could not read, but the huge parking lot contained many buses. Riobamba!

Whether meeting the black eyes of the Tuareqs of West Africa hiding behind turbans wrapped around their heads and faces, or the welcoming tourist-oriented Indians of San Blas, you will encounter experiences not found in textbooks that will prepare you for the life that awaits you.

What a role our memories play as they lay the foundation for the building blocks of everything yet to come. You do not weigh incredible memories by the ingredients of one experience. Our reactions when meeting new people can turn on the magic.

We take unconscious notes and recognize their import later as we recall the impact people make on our attitudes. As our own expectations of ourselves grow, our confidence and strengths reveal themselves. The real substance lives not around us but within.

Erasing past commitments, your capacity for new circumstances, different ways of viewing the world and making new friendships will grow. By practicing new skills, you will enhance your aptitude for brainstorming new ideas and becoming more self-sufficient. Once you have made a personal connection with a foreign culture, you will change forever.

ADJUST YOUR EYES TO WIDE OPEN WHILE TRAVELING

You will open many doors while traveling, and sometimes may come to a door that makes you wonder if you have the strength to push through it. Take care in your responses to the uniqueness of people and their curious customs. Remember, you do not TAKE your photographs and stories. You BORROW them! Let them reflect the soul of your new friends.

Find favorable circumstances to help bridge that gap between your country's lifestyle and the ways of foreign ancestors' past. While sharpening the edges of your new adventure, fill your beliefs about those of this new culture with compassion.

Magnify their traditions and stories from the past with compliments. Travel plans seldom play out as expected so remember this: Flexibility and patience will help save the day.

Value your health and safety while, at the same time, you comprehend the meaning of the cliché phrase that the journey exceeds the importance of the destination.

Open the windows wide and breathe in all that you see. Meeting with new cultures will compel you to value the grand diversity of the places we, as humans, call home.

Neither guidebooks nor teachers in classrooms nor even experience on the road can hand you the skills of travel. Travel accomplishments stem from our emotional reactions. What we take from the experience helps to transform us.

"Once you have traveled, the voyage never ends, but is played out over and over again in the quietest chambers that the mind can never break off from the journey." Pat Conroy

Images by Chapter: Order by Code & Caption

AdventureTravelPress.com   Available: color, B/W, all sizes: see website

	Image Code	**Caption**
Ethiopia		
1	E-156-11	Hammar tribal planting corn
2	E-151-27	Tsamy walking from Konso wearing animal skins
3	E-150-18A	Mursi without her lip disc
4	E-151-11	Carrying market purchase
5	E-151-16	Tribal man carrying his rifle
6	E-191-07s	Children playing in the market area
7	E-161-06s	Lip disc on Mursi woman
8	E-165-18s	Mursi men in loincloths blocking path with AK47s
9	E-161-03s	Mursi playing handmade musical instrument
10	E-166-6s	Young girls selling gourds
11	E-170-22s	Galeb tribal dressed in animal skins
12	E-173-29s	Digging for water in a dry riverbed
13	E-156-20	Cooking inside hut
14	E-172-22s	Cooking oxen dung to drink
15	E-166-08	Boy carving neck stools
16	E-171-14s	Grinding maize on a stone
17	E-167-33s	The leaky purple tent
18	E-174-34s	Wrapping bundles of firewood
19	E-172-36s	Tribal boys tasting author's leftover spaghetti for first time
20	E-191-19s	Painting faces at the well
21	E-156-18	Turmi children skinning a goat for food
22	E-154-12	Hammar woman carrying a heavy load
23	E-175-04s	Proud and beautiful tribal woman
24	E-194-08s	Oxen plowing
25	E-166-03s	Selling gourds in tribal market
26	E-166-31s	Tribal friends gathered in market
27	E-190-05s	Berber women from Somalia
28	E-170-08s	Scraps patch worked into a hut
29	E-170-32s	Author talking with Galeb children
30	E-155-16	Karo sisters pumping water from local Konso well
31	E-155-25	Karo girls shave their heads until they pass through puberty
32	E-153-14	Hammar teenager with shaved head resting Demeka market
33	E-166-29s	Painted faces

www.ingramcontent.com/pod-product-compliance
Lightning Source LLC
Chambersburg PA
CBHW041752040426
42446CB00001B/17